WILL NOT WORK FOR FOOD

9 BIG IDEAS For Effectively Managing Your Business In An Increasingly Dumb, Distracted & Dishonest America

Clay Clark

U.S. Small Business Administration Entrepreneur of the Year, U.S. Chamber National Blue Ribbon Quality Award Winner, Metro Chamber of Commerce Young Entrepreneur of the Year, Business Consultant / Speaker of Choice for Fortune 500 Companies and Countless Businesses From Coast To Coast

ISBN 978-0-9984435-9-1

Radically change how you approach management to experience results like Disney, Apple, Chik-Fil-A, Southwest, and QuikTrip.

I n a time when news stories and media outlets are focused daily around the national unemployment statistics, Clay Clark asks the tough questions that very few seem to be asking when it comes to the nation's struggling employment figures. Is it really possible that over 10% of the American population is really too dishonest, too dumb, and too distracted to be employable? Could it really be the Harvard Business Review found more people quit jobs than were fired from jobs amidst this severe recession? Could it really be true in an ultracompetitive time of globalization where many companies are debating whether they should outsource jobs or not, the work ethic of America's workforce is at an all-time low? Could we simply have over 10% of the American population who would prefer to be unemployed in order to cash their government checks? And if the statistics, facts and figures don't lie, how are America's top companies dealing with a workforce where over 10% of the employees are dangerously dumb, deliberately dishonest, and disturbingly distracted?

How do top companies such as Disney, Apple, Chik-Fil-A, Southwest, and QuikTrip continue to thrive while many American companies just struggle to survive? In this controversial management guide, Clark points out the "Elephant In the Room" plaguing the American economy while providing the action steps all business owners and entrepreneurs need to know when it comes to effectively managing in a dumb, dishonest, and distracted America.

As a successful serial entrepreneur and one of the nation's top business consultants, Clark has literally spent thousands of hours consulting in the baking, basketball, college / university, commercial real estate, entertainment, fitness, fundraising, graphic design, identification badge, insurance, landscaping, legal services marketing, limousine, medical, mortgage, nutrition supplementation, paint, personal development, photography, salon, search engine optimization, social media, trade show, technology, web design, and video production industries. Clark has entertained and educated nearly 1,500 audiences since 1999 including Bama Companies, Farmers Insurance, Hewlett Packard, QuikTrip, and Valspar Paint.

Using insights and relevant data from his first-hand consulting experiences, credible research studies, and his own businesses, Clark provides the American entrepreneur with a practical and proactive approach to managing employees effectively in an increasingly dumb, dishonest, and distracted America. The "10 BIG IDEAS" he teaches in this book have the power to absolutely revolutionize your company's profitability, productivity, and overall performance.

By using the winning best-practice strategies found within *Will Not Work For Food,* you can dramatically increase your profitability and the overall success of your organization. Any business hiring and firing employees can learn and quickly implement the action-steps and principles found within this book to produce outstanding results, and complete dominance within their industry. This book will challenge you and make you laugh as you learn what you need to know to grow your organization in a time when a large number of Americans are unemployable.

Clay Clark is the business consultant, entertainer and educator of choice for many of the World's top companies including Bama Companies, Farmers Insurance, Hewlett Packard, QuikTrip, and Valspar Paints. As the "Tulsa Metro Chamber of Commerce Young Entrepreneur of the Year" at age 20 and the "U.S. Small Business Administration Entrepreneur of the Year" at age 27, Clark is a popular workshop leader and keynote speaker for many of the nation's top brands. Clark lives in Tulsa Oklahoma with his wife, four daughters and son.

Table of Contents

Preface

With All Due Respect, Before We Offend 30% of the Population with Facts, Let's Look at What Those Mean Numbers Tell Us

A few times in my life I've been physically heavy. During those times, when I have asked people the question, "Do I look fat?" some people have responded by saying, "No, you look great." The ones who said I "look great" are liars. However, Jolene Otteson, who said, "Clay, you look fat" was mean. Because of "Mean Jolene" I lost a bunch of weight and got in great shape just to spite her. Jolene was caring enough to be candid and for that I thank her. Because Jolene chose not to showcase "false kindness" with me, I was able to make actual changes in my real life.

I believe that today in America we all need a "Mean Jolene" who cares enough to sit down with us to discuss reality as it is; not as we wish it to be. And so for the rest of this book, I will be America's "Mean Jolene."

To say that this generation of American employees is the least intelligent, the most dishonest, and the most distracted generation in American history would be mean. It would be even harsher to say that this generation of American employees is the most sexually promiscuous, financially clueless, work ethic deprived, morally bankrupt, chronically disinterested, academically challenged, sexually transmitted disease ridden, and most over-college educated group of idiots ever assembled. However, NOTHING IS MORE HARSH than knowing that the above statements are based on facts and that you, as an employer, have to hire these people to make your businesses run smoothly and profitably.

Do you remember when childhood was supposed to be about exploration, love, and innocence? They don't.

- A study put together in 2006 by the Centers for Disease Control and Prevention showed that 1 in 4 women and 1 in 6 men were sexually abused before the age of 18. This means there are more than 42 million adult survivors of child sexual abuse in the United States.

Did your father ever tell you what it meant to be a man or a woman? Their fathers didn't.

- According to research conducted by the U.S. Census Bureau and posted on Fatherhood.org, nearly 24 million children in America (1 out of 3) live in homes where the biological father is absent..
- According to a study done by the Fulton County Texas Department of Corrections, 85% of all youths in prison come from fatherless homes. Thus, kids who come from fatherless homes are nearly 20 times more likely to go to jail than kids who were raised in a home with their biological fathers.
- According to a September 1988 study by the United States Department of Justice, 70% of youths in state-operated institutions come from fatherless homes – 9 times the average.

Did you ever get in trouble with your parents for not studying hard and doing well on your tests? They never did.

- In a 2011 article written Lory Hough, the Harvard School of Education found that over 50% of the 18-24

year old Americans surveyed by National Geographic couldn't find the state of New York on a map.
- In a Sept 14, 2011 article posted by Michael Winter for *USA Today*, the College Board now shows that just 40% of the high school seniors met benchmarks for college success.

Did your parents ever teach you about the consequences of your actions? Their parents never did.

- In a May of 2008 article published in *USA Today*, researchers in Chicago found that 1 in 4 teen girls have a sexually transmitted disease. Thus, approximately 3 million teens now have an STD.
- In a March 9th, 2012 article posted on *Reuters* by JoAnne Allen, about 16% of Americans between the ages of 14 and 49 are infected with genital herpes, making it one of the most common sexually transmitted diseases.
- In *Newsweek's* cover story entitled "iCrazy", it was revealed that one quarter of employees who use the internet during work visit porn sites. In fact, hits to porn sites are highest during office hours than at any other time of day.

Did your parents tell you not to lie? Their parents never did.

- 40% of the information on résumés is misrepresented (false, untrue, a lie) according to research conducted by American DataBank from 2008 - 2010.

Did your parents ever teach you that a quitter never wins and that a winner never quits? Their parents never did.

- Despite being in a deep economic recession, a July 7th, 2010 article published by the *Harvard Business Review* reported that more employees quit their jobs than were terminated, according to the US Bureau of Labor Statistics 3 month research.

Do you remember when college was supposed to make you more intelligent and more hirable? They don't.

- According to a *USA Today* Article written by Mary Beth Marklein, research shows students spent 50% less time studying compared with students a few decades ago. The research compared college students enrolled in 2001 versus college students enrolled in 2011.

Whatever happened to common sense?

- In a 2011 *Newsweek* Article, research was conducted by asking 1,000 U.S. citizens to take America's official citizenship test. Twenty nine percent (29%) couldn't name the Vice President. Seventy-three percent couldn't correctly explain why we fought the Cold War.
- According to Gail Cunningham, spokeswoman for the National Foundation of Credit Counseling, as quoted in a July 2012 article in *Newsweek* Magazine, 56% of U.S. adults admit they don't have a budget; one-third don't pay all their bills on time.
- According to an article written by Mary Beth Marklein in *USA Today*, nearly half of the nation's undergraduates show almost no gains in learning in their first two years of college. The report concludes

this is because, in large part, colleges don't make academics a priority. Among their top activities, students report spending 24% of their time sleeping, 51% of their time socializing and just 7% actually studying.

If you work hard and commit yourself to excellence anyone can obtain the American dream. But what if you don't want to work hard?

Free Bonus Tip: *"Nothing will work unless you do." - Maya Angelou (Poet, producer, actress and prolific writer)*

- In a study published in *Inc. Magazine* in June of 2007 and written by Liz Webber, research showed that average employees wasted an average of 1.7 hours of an 8.5 hour workday, while 20-29 year olds wasting 2.1 hours per day.
- A LEADERSHIPIQ study of 6,000 workers featured on *Fox News* in 2008 revealed that in 2008 nearly 25% of the average American's workday was wasted. Thus, the average employee was reported to waste nearly 2.3 hours per day.
- In a February 22, 2010 article featured in *Inc. Magazine* and written by Kim Boatman research conducted by SpectorSoft Corp, concluded that 89% of the businesses that were studied discovered employees were wasting time or abusing Internet use.
- In an article posted on Salary.com by Aaron Goveia in 2012, a study showed almost two-thirds of employees admitted to wasting time at work on the computer each day. The next obvious question is, how much time?

Do you remember what it was like to converse with someone who wasn't updating their Facebook status and texting while waiting for you to finish speaking? They don't.

- According to research conducted by Research Basex and reported in a February issue of *USA Today*, "productivity losses due to the cost of unnecessary interruptions" were at $650 billion in 2007.
- In a 2002 article published by NY Times Best-Selling Author Ken Blanchard, a large survey of 1,300 private-sector companies, conducted by Proudfoot Consulting, found that on average only 59% of work time is productive.
- A March 2, 2011 study published by *Inc. Magazine* reports that employees are unproductive for half of the day.
- In an article posted by Martha C. White on March 13th, 2012 entitled, "You're Wasting Time at Work Right Now, Aren't You?" revealed that a 2012 study of 3,200 employees conducted by Salary.com showed that 64% say they visit websites unrelated to work daily.

Do you remember when 1 out of 5 of your co-workers wasn't insane? They don't.

- According to a disturbing article published by *Harvard Health Publications* in February of 2010, researchers analyzing results from the U.S. National Co-morbidity Survey found a nationally representative study of Americans ages 15 to 54. In that study it was reported that 18% of those who were employed said they experienced symptoms of a mental health disorder in the previous month.

Introduction

The Overall Mindset of the "Will Not Work for Food" People

"The last thing I want to do is hurt you.
But it's still on my list."
- 30% of the American Workforce

In 2008, while watching the vigorous televised debates featuring the poetic, witty, and academic Senator Barack Obama versus the obstinate and proudly patriotic pragmatic Senator John McCain, I literally could not stop laughing. As an American entrepreneur, I found myself tickled to the core as both candidates shamelessly played to the crowd. The candidates couldn't agree on much but they both seemed hell bent on convincing us all that "today, America has the best workers in the world!" Their campaign commercials echoed this delusional optimism day after day. At one point Senator McCain even ran a series of political ads that said, "You, the American workers, are the best in the world. But your economic security has been put at risk by the greed of Wall Street. That's unacceptable."

- **Verify this insanity at:**
  http://blogs.wsj.com/numbersguy/ranking-the-workers-of-the-world-416/

If an American small business owner were running for office they would probably say, "70% of you, the American workers, are the best in the world. But your economic security has been put at risk by your dumb, dishonest, and distracted coworkers. That's unacceptable."

I travel around the country teaching companies of various sizes the "best practice business systems" they need to incorporate to grow in nearly every kind of industry imaginable. During my travels I continue to hear countless stories about the laughable work ethic of nearly half of "American workers." As I continue to run my own companies I also continue to find myself shocked by the idiocy of nearly 50% of the "American workers" and job applicants.

During my first five years in business I used to think that I was the only business owner in America who found myself surrounded by dumb, dishonest, and distracted employees. I thought because I had chosen to start a wedding entertainment business, this was the price I was going to have to pay. However, in 2007, due to the success of our businesses, I was named by the U.S. Small Business Administration "Entrepreneur of the Year" for the State of Oklahoma. Quickly, from that point on, I found myself getting requests for numerous consulting jobs in a variety of industries ranging from the jewelry business, lending, insurance, to commercial real estate and beyond. As I visited each business across the country I was shocked to find the same "dumb, dishonest, and distracted" behavior at nearly every business I visited. It didn't matter whether I was in Wisconsin working with teachers or in Miami, Florida working with high-level financial planners. The "dumb, dishonest, and distracted" workers were everywhere, except at the top companies.

At first I almost kind of enjoyed the camaraderie and the kinship I was able to share with each business owner I met. As an entrepreneur you often find yourself alone at the top of company hierarchy; many of them semi-therapeutically enjoyed sharing their prolific stories of employee incompetence with me after spending a day vigorously focusing on improving their core business systems. For them, as they shared their stories it was therapeutic; for me, it was hilariously sad.

One business owner told me of a mortgage consultant that consistently asked pregnant and not-so-pregnant larger women, "When is your baby due?" as his rapport building question of choice to prospective clients looking to refinance their homes. One entrepreneur / business owner nervously shared with me how he routinely had to remind his employees that they were not allowed to look at "pornography on their smartphones during working hours." One hard working home builder in Ohio explained to me that he had "one of his top employees" call in "because he wanted to know if he could take another sick day to treat the infections that resulted from him getting a really awesome full-sleeve tattoo." Yet another business owner nervously asked me, "How do you handle situations where a current employee is having sex with and is trying to date the new female employee whom we just recruited and whom he just met two days ago?" Another name-brand retailer asked me, "How do you recommend I manage an employee who routinely shows up more than two hours late to work?" Where are the "best workers in the world" that Senator Obama and Senator McCain spoke so highly about in their campaign speeches? Could it be that nearly 30% of the American population is unemployable? Could it be that Detroit has been decimated financially because they have one of the worst workforces in the world?

To further highlight this epidemic of "idiocracy" that is sweeping our nation, whenever I ask these employers why they don't just fire these terrible employees they explain to me that "I want to fire them, but they are the best people I can find right now." Whenever I have dared to peel back the onion of employee-related questioning, I usually receive even more shocking responses. Just before throwing up their hands, many entrepreneurs and business owners will say, "Look, I really do want to hire great employees, but these are the only people I can find that can pass a drug test and don't have a tattoo on their neck!"

Every time I hear these stories part of me wants to laugh hysterically at the absolute absurdity of the situation, and another part of me wants to cry. However, because I owe a tremendous amount of my success to being a delusional optimist, I have decided to write a book dedicated to providing practical solutions for effectively managing in a dumb, dishonest, and distracted America.

This book may make you laugh and cry while asking yourself, "Why!? Why?! Why?!" But after you have read this book I promise that you will find yourself feeling empowered and inspired by the action steps that result from implementing the *8 Secrets to Effectively Manage in a Dumb, Dishonest, and Distracted America.*

In order for you to take your business to the next level, we must first start by being honest with ourselves. This is important because if we're not honest, the customer most certainly will be. As entrepreneurs and business owners we all must ask ourselves the tough questions:

- If I was a customer, would I appreciate receiving a service from my current employees?
- If I was a customer, would I feel like my employees inspire, or erode, confidence in the products that we produce?
- How smart are my employees as demonstrated by their ability to solve problems?
- How honest are my employees with me on a consistent basis?

- How much time per day do my employees waste away on their non work-related technology such as Twitter, Facebook, Instant Messaging, YouTube, Google+, etc?
- What percentage of my employees are top performers and what percentage of my employees are bottom feeders?
- If I was putting together a team of people to solve a big problem, would I hire my employees?
- If I was a customer, would I become passionate, or pessimistic, about the overall financial well-being of the company after interacting with my employees?
- How well can my employees spell?
- How much time am I wasting on training employees how to do the basics because my current employees don't grasp the fundamentals of reading, writing, and basic arithmetic?

You see, during many of the consulting talks I give all around the country, just asking these questions has had the ability to inspire employers to become an enemy of mediocrity in their businesses. Over the years I have literally witnessed companies triple in size within a year simply by replacing terrible employees with good ones. However, here are the brutal realities that you and I have to face day in and day out if we are truly committed to producing sensational products (and services) and extraordinary profits:

- America can now be divided into two groups, the employable and the unemployable.
- From my experience working with companies across the country I firmly believe that two-thirds of all Americans are employable. The man or woman who shows up to work on-time every day has now been promoted to "management material" status. The person

who actually does their job without suing their employer is now a modern day "miracle worker".

- The employee who decides to not bring their personal drama to the workplace is now being revered as the office "self-help guru" and the kind of person that companies fight over.
- Many of the employees that currently make up America's workforce simply go from job to job suing employers, calling-in-sick, bringing drama to the workplace, perpetually showing up late, and disrespecting their supervisor and those around them. These people take endless smoke breaks, consider gambling to be an "investment," and consider Kim Kardashian to be a hero.

Although this information provides considerable job security to those involved in ministries and homeless outreaches, it can be a little disheartening to you and I as managers, business owners, and entrepreneurs if we are not careful.

So With Incompetent Employees Now the Norm, What Are Success-Focused Entrepreneurs and Business Owners To Do?

Well, we have some good news and some bad news here. On the bad side, unfortunately, nearly 30% of all of the people you meet will be dumb, dishonest, or distracted. On a positive note, you can win simply by getting them out of your office and into your competition's office.

As you look for and manage new employees keep Sam Walton's famous words in mind, *"There is only one boss. The customer. And he can fire anybody in the company from the chairman on down simply by spending his money somewhere else."*

As you manage people remember what Steve Jobs said, "*Be a yardstick of quality. Some people aren't used to an environment where excellence is expected.*"

When you head into your next staff meeting keep Lee Cockerell, the former Senior Operating Executive of Disney who managed 40,000 plus cast members, in mind. He advised, "*You should expect what you allow.*"

Chapter One

BIG IDEA #1: How Did America Became Dumb,
Dishonest, & Distracted
(The Shift from a Democracy to an Idiocracy)

When did we transform from a democracy to an idiocracy? When did we replace real heroes like Nelson Mandela, Abraham Lincoln, Vince Lombardi, and the Reverend Martin Luther King, Jr. with potentially demon-possessed or dumb heroes like Lil' Wayne, Octo-Mom, Kim Kardashian, and Robert Downey Jr.? Just turn on any news station for 30 minutes or less and you are almost guaranteed to come across some news story announcing the newest unemployment numbers and some new sex tape that has been released by some American celebrity. "Too many jobs are being outsourced" one talking head will say. "America simply cannot compete with cheap foreign labor" another will say. A conservative voice and "economic expert" will quickly look for a way to blame President Obama for the "poor unemployment outlook." A liberal "economic analyst" no doubt will find a way to blame a greedy American entrepreneur for being a "cold-blooded capitalist hell bent on profits regardless of the damage they are doing to the American economy." Then a talking head will come on and talk about the Lil' Wayne's most recent drug sentence, the legacy of 2Pac and what drug this celebrity or that celebrity is on.

It's amazing to me that the concept of America's deteriorating ideals is not discussed more often in the media. Although the unemployment stats get talked about every day, the "elephant in the room" for most of today's businesses is that nearly half of our workforce is either dumb, dishonest, or distracted. American kids are now growing up hoping to become the next "Teen Mom" star on MTV and the next face-tattooed rapper like Lil' Wayne. As our country has systematically replaced our role models, we have also attempted to tear down the credibility of people with integrity. Bill Cosby gets written off as old and no longer relevant simply because he challenges an African American community where 75% of the children are born in single parent homes. Franklin Graham quickly gets labeled as a bigot and Tim Tebow gets used as a national punching bag for pundits who love bashing "judgmental Christians" who chose to refrain from having sex with anything that moves.

- **Verify this insanity by going to your local mall. Sit, watch, and take notes. There are idiots everywhere.**

As our country has begun promoting this next generation of heroes, the schools are pumping out an army of morons into the marketplace. Colleges and online universities are sending out confused people into the workforce that are incredibly dumb, morally deprived, and disengaged from living a life filled with any semblance of meaning. Many companies are now being forced to fire people because they demand high wages for terrible work. A large number of the clients I work with simply refuse to drive American automobiles because their experience has taught them it's better not to drive a vehicle that was built by a dumb, dishonest, and distracted employee.

Forget China, forget inflation, forget the "gloom and doom" economic reports. Many of America's business leaders are being forced to fire people just because they are incompetent. Unlike previous generations where most people had much of their stupidity and rebellion scared out of them by Dad at home, today the majority of Americans are growing up without a Dad at home. Just take a look at the incarceration statistics and you will quickly discover the link between absent fathers and absent minded adults. Whether it's a poor education system or just a poor mindset, people are truly getting less intelligent. Consider the fact that a *Newsweek* poll discovered that nearly 25% of the population has no idea who the Vice President of our country is. Consider that fact that the majority of our country is unaware that buying a car with credit means that they will have to pay for the car nearly twice before they make their final payment. It's truly astonishing how many people have no concept of what factors into a car loan. We now live in a country where studies are showing that people are more familiar with *American Idol* than they are with who is running for President of the United States.

Time and again I hear, "Today we had to let someone go" and "Last week we had to let someone go." These are the kinds of things I keep encountering as I travel around the country teaching "best-practice" business skills to today's business leaders. Whether it's a major food manufacturer or a local small business, virtually every day companies all over the country are being forced to "let people go" because of their lack of competence. Today, before I wrote this portion of the book I physically watched in shock as the Office Manager for one of my clients updated her Facebook and responded to at least a half dozen non work-related text messages during and before an office meeting. This person had no fear of being caught and actually did this activity openly; right in front of her boss. This person then went on to explain during the meeting that they didn't have time to get all of their work done this week. Sure, some layoffs are related to jobs being shipped overseas; however, many times these employers are not being forced to let people go because the economy is bad. They are being forced to let people go because they are terrible employees.

I've literally had conversations with home-builders, call center operators, print shop owners, and numerous business owners who have said, "I can't find a decent American worker anywhere! I sincerely believe that in order to make it, we are going to have to hire illegal workers from other countries if we can't find some decent American workers soon."

Countless HR Directors across the country have told me that around one-third of the people who apply for jobs at their company tell them that they "really don't want to start working until their unemployment runs out." Are you kidding me? These same HR Directors have told me that more people are quitting their jobs than are losing their jobs due to layoff or job elimination. It's truly astonishing and mind-boggling when you speak with these HR Directors. Today's business leaders have to let people go because they are managing morons who check their social media updates every 5 minutes. Companies are being forced to fire people because they won't stop texting back and forth with their boyfriend long enough to get anything done. My friends, whenever I ask these HR Directors, "What's the biggest limiter on your business's growth?" I nearly always hear, "If you could find some people that were honest and who actually showed up on time, we could be growing by leaps and bounds."

Dealing with Dumb Employees
"Whenever I watch TV and see those poor starving kids all over the world, I can't help but cry. I mean I'd love to be skinny like that but not with all those flies and death and stuff."
- Mariah Carey, pop singer

4

Consider this: Research reported in the *New York Times* reports that currently 45% of people who have attended college for two years are for the first time showing no improvements in their cognitive or critical thinking skills.

- **Verify this insanity at:**
  http://opinionator.blogs.nytimes.com/2011/09/21/what-do-test-scores-tell-us/

At the middle school and high school level, kids are supposed to learn how to learn. As more and more technology is introduced into the classroom, less and less teaching is done. Teachers are simply clicking through an endless series of multi-media presentations on their "fancy" technology presentation boards while students are listening to Lil' Wayne on their iPhones. The teacher's job of instructing, challenging, and inspiring students has now been replaced with their new job of babysitting, breaking up fights, taking attendance, and managing the kids in a "politically correct way." Large numbers of teachers I've spoken to have told me that they spend well over half of their time dealing with behavior problems and what's left of their time is now spent teaching the students anything.

Dealing with Distracted Employees
Distracted Driving Kills People, Distracted Workers Kill Your Bottom Line

We all know that research clearly shows that distracted driving kills people. It's a little tough to focus on driving while sending an intense text to your ex or to turn while attempting to learn what happened at yesterday's meeting via text. We all know how frustrating it can be to watch a movie with someone who won't quit asking questions while the film is showing or how maddening it can be to golf with someone who keeps taking cell phone calls while you're attempting to putt.

However, businesses throughout the country are paying employees who are completely mentally disengaged from the workplace. Joe is texting Sally about dinner plans, the upcoming game, and home drama on your time and all of the time. Countless research is now revealing that between non-work related emails and texts, smoke breaks, and social media, videogames, nearly 40% of the average employee's workday is spent doing something other than working. And again, nearly half of those people are already struggling with being dumb and dishonest.

- **Verify this insanity at:**
  http://www.usatoday.com/tech/columnist/kimkomando/
  story/2012-02-24/work-monitor-
  smartphone/53221804/1

Although the information above makes me want to staple my forehead out of frustration, I am sincerely encouraged by your ability to break out of the clutter of commerce. This can be accomplished if you will simply devote yourself to studying successful companies and doing what they have done to build their billionaire dollar brands. However, because I know that you are too busy to devote ten years of your life to reading case studies to develop the action plans as I have done, the rest of this book is dedicated to providing you with the proven and practical plans used by America's biggest and most loved brands. In this uncertain economic environment brands including Disney, QuikTrip, Chik-Fil-A, Southwest Airlines, Apple, and other companies are still producing BIG RESULTS by implementing these plans; and now you can too!

Dealing with Dishonest Employees
Will Your Stuff Still Be There When Your Employee Goes Home For the Night?

Assuming that you have found an employee that doesn't have a coy fish tattoo on their neck and that shows up on time, you still wouldn't be in the clear yet; unless you are ok with them stealing all of your profits. According to a study conducted by the U.S. Chamber of Commerce and published in *Inc. Magazine,* one-third of all business bankruptcies are a result of theft in the workplace. This is insane to me. Shouldn't this be talked about? To me, one-third is an absurdly large percentage. Wow! Please excuse me as I deal with my nausea.

- **Verify this insanity at:**
  http://www.inc.com/articles/1999/05/13731.html

As America's youth continues to replace role models with those who are famous for their roles in sex tapes, the overall standards of our country are lowering. Kids are now basing their moral standards on the morality displayed by the morons they look up to like Lil' Wayne and other celebrity idiots. These people are famous for tattooing their face, rapping about having sex with random people, and getting arrested for possessing more pot than a Mexican drug cartel. The overall American pop culture is teaching kids who have grown up without fathers that morality is all about doing what feels good at the time. Artists like 50 Cent and athletes like Mark McGuire have told this generation of fatherless kids through their actions that lying, cheating, and stealing is totally fine if that's what you have to do to get where you want to go, i.e., to become famous and set records in professional sports.

My friends, morality is no longer common. In fact "common sense" is no longer common. Whether we endorse the downward spiral of America's morals or not, you must accept the reality that at least ¼ of your employees are lying to you, stealing from you, or cheating you in some way. To prevent yourself from getting robbed blind you must embrace Ronald Reagan's philosophy of "trust but verify". You simply cannot afford not to.

Because I understand that most entrepreneurs feel alone at the top of their business mountain, I thought it would be therapeutic to conclude this introduction and to segue into the rest of the book with a list of many of the dishonest excuses for not performing that some dishonest employees have actually said to me over the years. Although they all irritated me to the point that I wanted to crush their dishonest skulls at the time, I must admit that some of these really do make me laugh now when I look at the idiocy on display in their statements.

"Hey boss, what's the policy on calling in sick? I feel really terrible this morning; it must have been something I ate." - Found out later that the dishonest employee was so drunk the night before that he couldn't walk.

"No, this coat is not Jason's coat. I know it looks like Jason's coat, but it is not Jason's coat." - Later we discovered that this employee actually had the audacity to steal the coat and wallet from a coworker. This moron then had the lack of a soul needed to actually wear this stolen coat to work every day; while actually sitting within fifteen feet of the person from whom he had stolen the coat and wallet.

"Hey Clay, I wanted to call in because I'm at the hospital with my mom who has cancer." - Found out later that he was at a strip club every time he said that "he was at the hospital with his mom who had cancer."

"Clay I've literally made over 100 calls per day every day this week to our prospective clients. I think people just don't want to buy because the economy is so tough." - Found out later that he was calling his girlfriend and the same business over and over nearly 300 times within 6 days in order to "fake" his call numbers.

"Clay I realize that the gas bill was THREE TIMES more than normal, but that is just because the gas prices went up." - We later discovered by doing some basic math that a twelve cent per gallon increase in the cost of gas had not tripled the cost of gas. After doing further research we discovered that the employee had filled his boat up with gas using the company credit card.

"Boss, I think it's cool that your friend is a pop star. I don't know if you know this, but I was actually in a band back in the day. In fact, I'm a phenomenal singer." - Only after we forced him to sing through relentless peer pressure did he fess up to the fact that he was a liar who was never in a band.

"Hey man, I have definitely taken out the trash every day this week." - We later discovered that the employee had not taken out the trash in three weeks when a plague of fruit flies descended upon us like the plague of death.

"Dude you know that I am totally not the kind of guy that would screw you. I'm telling you, I drove around for like three hours looking for the place." - Found out the employee actually just decided to skip work that day so that he could go out on a date.

"The traffic is unbelievable here on the highway!" - We soon discovered a pathological liar in our midst when this employee ran into traffic every week for 9 weeks in a row before we could fire him.

"I promise that I have mailed everything out on time. Seriously, I've never mailed anything late; it must be FedEx and UPS." - We found out that this employee, who actually had the audacity to blame both UPS and FedEx for his incompetence, had never actually mailed any of the documents he was referring to on time.

"I always call the clients back. Those four people must just be weird." - We soon discovered that this employee also had over 15 unchecked voicemails dating back as far as one month.

"Boss, I didn't know that we had a 'no sunflower seed eating' policy in the office. You guys are always changing stuff without telling me." - These comments were made after it was discovered that they were spitting sunflower seeds under their desk on the sales floor in the office.

"Sir, I would never compete with you. In fact, I would never run a business that competes with you after all you have done for me." - Discovered later that this person had been systematically telling all of our loyal customers that he was leaving our company because we were drug addicts and he felt like he could no longer be a part of our team. The irony of the situation is that he was the one who was actually fired for drug use.

"I've been using the system every week and it just doesn't work. It's really disheartening because I've been putting my heart into it and I've never seen any results." - We found out later that he had never actually done the marketing activities and had actually gone through the effort of systematically lying to us at every juncture to justify his laziness.

Chapter Two

BIG IDEA #2 - Hire Only A & B Players

B efore I begin teaching you the irrefutable truth that YOUR COMPANY CAN THRIVE ONLY IF YOU COMMIT TO RECRUITING AND EMPLOYING "A AND B PLAYERS" ONLY, let's take a brief time out to assume that I don't know what I'm talking about. Let's assume for a moment that you, as the reader, don't value my opinion as a consultant, author, and business owner. If that's the case, whom would you believe? Whose opinion would you value? As a general rule most people only value people who have demonstrated verifiable and profound levels of success. So to prove my point I'm going to start off this chapter by letting you see what the gurus had to say about managing humans.

- "Be a yardstick of quality. Some people aren't used to an environment where excellence is expected."- Steve Jobs (Revolutionary Founder of Apple)
- "As we became leaner, we found ourselves communicating better, with fewer interpreters and fewer filters. We found that with fewer layers we had wider spans of management. We weren't managing better. We were managing less, and that was better." - Jack Welch (Iconic former CEO of GE)
- "People who are unable to get things done must be fired. At Trump our value is based upon the "You can

make excuses or you can make money"- Donald Trump (Real Estate Mogul, Author, and the man behind the *TRUMP* brands)

- "If you aren't fired up with enthusiasm, you'll be fired with enthusiasm." - Vince Lombardi (Legendary *National Football League* Hall of Fame coach)
- "Lazy hands make a man poor, but diligent hands bring wealth." - Proverbs 10:4 (New International Version)

You have to grasp this concept of business, otherwise you will be unable to thrive and you will always find yourself struggling to merely survive. Trust me on this. I have personally enabled enough morons to fill up a casting call for an average rap video many times over. This was not a good thing and I paid the price for allowing these under-performing "C Players" to call my office home. You simply cannot afford to have any "C Players" on your team. They will occupy your time with mindless justifications for lack or performance and destroy your ability to deliver your products and services to your customers at a high level. These people also emit dangerously contagious amounts of negativity to everyone they come in contact with. If they aren't killing your motivation with their stories of woe, they will kill the motivation of the person next to them as they complain about the "unrealistic expectations" that you place on everyone.

"If you accept the expectations of others, especially negative ones, then you never will change the outcome." - Michael Jordan (National Basketball Association Hall of Fame player)

Hire only A & B Players by focusing on hiring for attitude and training skills. The day to day drama will decrease while the quality of your products and services will increase dramatically. At the end of the day when it all comes down to it, you just can't surround yourself with people that can't get the job done. Jack Welch, the former CEO and the iconic leader of GE, was famous for looking for employees that had what he called the "4 E's." Every time he hired anyone he looked for individuals who had the ability to bring ENERGY to the workplace, the ability to ENERGIZE others, the ability to EXECUTE the business plans to get things done, and the EDGE needed to be candid with everyone at all times.

In the rare case that someone was actually able to deliver high marks in all four of his "4 E" areas, he referred to them as "A" players. If someone was great in a couple of areas, but lacking in others he referred to them as "B" players. When someone was weak in every area, he called them "C" players; then he called them into his office and fired them.

Friend, the harsh reality of business is that customers in a capitalist society are not patient. Why should they be? If your product or service is terrible they are simply going to find somewhere else to buy the product or service from a place with decent customer service. This competition and survival of the fittest is what makes our country great. Thus, if you want to make it big in this society, you must not tolerate the work of marginal "C Player" employees. "C Players" cannot be helped.

Psychologically, "A Players" love getting things done. They love wowing customers. They love results. They are purpose driven and they view mediocrity as a source of evil. People that don't get things done are an annoyance to them, so much so that many of them will refuse to stay at an organization where idiocy, lack of accountability, and excuses are the order of the day. If you don't want these top people going, you had better make sure that your organization is growing. "A Players" make up only 10-15% of all non-dumb, non-distracted, and non-dishonest employees; so you must work like hell to keep these people on your team or your organization will suffer.

"B Players" make up about 80% of every good workplace. These people value being part of the team and love being "consistent." They love showing up on time and leaving on time. They are not interested in staying late, nor are they very excited about anything that requires change. To them, "change is bad" and "consistency is good." They are unable to grasp the concept of incrementally improving a business to achieve peak results. However, they will reluctantly go along because they "don't want to rock the boat." Do not be annoyed by these people, because every organization needs "B Players". These employees value following the rules and honoring their word, but you cannot have your growth limited by their overall lack of ambition. Your goal as a leader should be to inspire, coach, and train your "B Players" into wanting to become "A Players". If you celebrate your "A Players" enough, some "B Players" will begin to become discontent with their current reality and will begin to act differently so that they too can join the ranks of your company's "A-Players".

"C Players" are negative and lazy. They are dumb, they are distracted, and they are dishonest. Their life's thermostat is permanently set to "make just enough money to support my baby's mamma" mode. These people spend their workday making excuses for not performing, talking bad about management, spreading rumors, and relentlessly questioning every aspect of your business. These people have decided to become full-time victims and they seek validation for their "mental disorders," "emotional situation they are going through," and for their "distractedness of late". These people are draining and they love to ask questions like, "Could you call me to remind me to wake up on time?" When they don't get something done they will always blame someone else. They can't write well because "their teachers in school weren't any good." They steal because "they had to make ends meet."

They'll routinely ask management "either/or" questions that don't make sense like:

- "So do you want me to be a good husband or a good salesman?"
- "Do you want me to get my paperwork done or to make my sales calls?"
- "Should I get everything done or focus on doing a good job?"

These people consistently make bad decisions but are unable to mentally grasp the concept that they ever caused any of the problems that they are currently experiencing in their lives. These people are "draining" and they will kill your business. When you "sit down" to meet with them they always find a way to make you feel responsible for their bad decisions and poor results. When dealing with these people, keep this quote by best-selling author and multi-millionaire businessman-turned-author, Harvey Mackey in mind, "It isn't the people you fire who make your life miserable, it's the people you don't fire."

Chapter Three

BIG IDEA #3: Inspire the People You Hire

O nce a human decides to come and work for you (this is entirely different if you hire a canine), it is your civic duty to inspire everyone whom you hire. Show me a great company and I will show you a leader who inspires their people. Show me an iconic brand everyone in America knows and I will show you a leadership team committed to keeping their people engaged on a daily basis. You simply cannot afford to overlook the importance of inspiring your people. Without inspiration your great new hires, whose heads were once filled with thoughts of motivation, will soon turn into disgruntled employees who are overwhelmed with thoughts of frustration. However, I know that you are a savvy business person and not the type of gullible person who considers a trip to the Casino to be an "investment" in your financial future. Therefore, I am going let you hear a few thoughts about the importance of inspiration and motivation from some of America's business leaders.

- "Expect more than others think possible." - Howard Schultz (The man who took Starbucks from small-time to big-time business)
- "We herd sheep, we drive cattle, we lead people. Lead me, follow me, or get out of my way." - George

S. Patton (One of the most famous military leaders of all time)
- "Effective leadership is putting first things first. Effective management is discipline, carrying it out. " - Stephen Covey (One of the most influential self-help authors in American history)
- "People don't care how much you know until they know how much you care." - John Maxwell (One of the world's leading leadership experts)

Now that you know you need to inspire your people, you are probably thinking, *Ok, that's great, but how do I do it?* This question is valid and it's why I'm going to give you "SIX MOVES" that you can use to inspire your people on a daily, weekly, annual, and decade-by-decade basis. However, in the spirit of transparency I must admit that none of these ideas are mine. I am just a relentless reader and an extremely focused implementer who has experienced success only because I am 100% committed to the concept of "being a pirate not a pioneer." My basic theory is based around my experience that when I study successful people and do what they do, then I begin to experience success as well. And so armed with the information that none of these "SIX MOVES" are mine, I need you to embrace them and to commit to acting upon them once you have determined which move is best for you. These "SIX MOVES" come from Tom's Shoes, Starbuck's Coffee, Apple, QuikTrip, Jack Welch's General Electric (not the GE Company or management systems of today) and Southwest Airlines.

MOVE #1 - Merge your company's philanthropic goals with your business and profitability goals.

By now I think that nearly every American on the planet is familiar with Tom's Shoes. I'm sure you are familiar with concept of "Buy a pair of Tom's Shoes and we will proudly donate a pair of shoes to a child in need from around the world." If you are not, take a moment and Google "Tom's Shoes." Check out their website and see genius, inspiration, and motivation at work within a big company. Tom's shoes went from being a small startup to a massive household name company at an incredibly fast pace. How did they find all of the good people needed to keep up with the growth? Tom's Shoes merged its philanthropic goals with the business and profitability goals of the company. Employees of Tom's feel like they are doing more than just selling shoes. They feel like they are making a difference; and they are. Tom's Shoes has great management systems and unbelievable PR savvy; yet it all comes back to their ability to convince their employees that their products are going to make a difference in the world in which they live. Tom's Shoes have even created a viral and cult-like following amongst their customers; who have also bought into this vision of being a change agent to make the world a better place simply by buying a pair of shoes.

To make this program work for you, here is what you need to do:

- Write out your specific philanthropic goals. Write down the specific people and organizations you would like to help.
- Determine what percentage of your company's profits you are willing to set aside to support these causes. Remember, Tom's Shoes gives a pair of shoes away for every pair of shoes that their customers purchase. However, this would not be possible if Tom's didn't decide to do this from the very beginning. Their entire pro forma and business model was built around the concept of doing this. Your company can do the same

thing if you are committed to a cause and passionate enough to see it through.

- Commit to sharing your philanthropic program with every customer and employee.
- Physically put your logo and your cause on every print piece, business card, sign, website, email, and piece of marketing material that you send out.
- Put in your company's monthly calendar to take a few moments to celebrate any of the positive impacts your team has made on the world as a result of your company's philanthropic program.

MOVE #2 - Set a goal that is so ambitious that it stretches your people on a daily basis.

When Howard Schultz came to Starbucks he had just finished taking time off from his corporate career to figure out what he wanted to do with the rest of his life. While traveling around the world he stumbled across people called "baristas" who ran these small little coffee shops that were all over Italy. These shops dominated the cities and were a central part of local Italian communities. People would gather at the shops to share stories and build relationships while enjoying a cup of coffee. Once he witnessed "baristas" at work at these small Italian coffee shops he was hooked. He became obsessed with the notion that every city in America would benefit greatly by having several of these local coffee shops. He knew that the crappy, burnt, and lukewarm coffee that Americans were choking down each morning to wake themselves up was not good enough. He knew that if he could truly recreate the ambiance and the aura of the little Italian coffee shops throughout America, it would work. He wasn't really concerned with how much it would cost or all of the reasons why it wouldn't work. He wasn't deterred that Americans were used to paying less than a dollar for their crappy coffee. He wasn't concerned that nothing like what he was talking about existed within the United States. He wasn't worried that he would have to introduce a concept, a store, a way of life, and a product into the marketplace. He was filled with a delusional optimism that was being brought about as a result of his passion for the product and service.

After quitting his comfortable white collar job to go to work for a small Seattle-based coffee shop, Schultz simply wouldn't stop talking about his desire create a "third place". He was obsessed with the concept of creating a place that wasn't home and it wasn't work, but it was uniquely Starbucks. He went from hoping that it would happen to committing to make it happen. His faith in his crazy plan to open multiple Starbucks stores in every American city drove the company to billion dollar business status and beyond. People bought into his vision because it was big, it was challenging, it was for the good of America, and he was sold out to it. My friend, if you have goals that are small and weak, no "A Players" are going to want to come and work for you. Nobody aspires to go to work someday for a stagnant, small, or medium sized business. Set a big vision that makes sense and that you are passionate about and just watch people get on board to help you.

To make this program work for you, here is what you need to do:

- Define the big goals for your company.
- Make certain that your company's big goals are known by everyone; all of the time. Put the big goal on your company's signage, on your business cards, on the walls, and every place where your employees congregate.
- Place specific, monthly times to share your company's big vision and where you are headed as a collective group with your staff.

MOVE #3 - Commit to creating incredible products that simply wow every one of your customers.

The late Steve Jobs was famous for being a jerk. People said he was mean. People said he was harsh. Today, Apple does not struggle with finding people who want to work with them. People naturally are attracted to the best of anything. Top people want to work where the best and most incredible products on the planet are designed, produced, and sold. People who own Apple products are so impressed with the packaging, presentation, service, and the products that Apple produces that many Americans now admit to keeping the boxes in which their computer came in. When was the last time you kept the box to your blender or TV because it was so cool? Never!

My friend, the iPhone changed the way people used their phone. Grizzly old dudes went from hating using their phone to loving to use their phones. Fifty-five year old moms who had never before been active with social media began posting Facebook status updates. Adults began using the phone because it was fun. This would not have been possible without Steve Jobs and his absolute maniacal obsession with making packaging, presentations, services, and products that people are passionate about. If the products Apple produced were anything less than amazing, no one would have wanted to work for a man with his erratic temper, foul mouth, and habit of stretching the truth to the point that even his closest colleagues began to label his way of thinking as the "reality distortion field." If you want people to flock to your business, demand excellence. You don't have to curse people out or display angry behavior in the workplace. You just have to been committed to wowing each and every customer and you will begin to attract some of the best and brightest minds in the world. As stated earlier, GREAT PEOPLE LOVE WORKING FOR GREAT COMPANIES THAT PRODUCE GREAT

PRODUCTS AND GREAT SERVICES. Great people struggle with feelings of guilt and dissonance when they work for a company that produces less than great work. Mediocre people are those that are offended by the accountability that is required to produce GREAT PRODUCTS and SERVICES.

To make this program work for you, here is what you need to do:

- Draw a line in the sand and let your employees know that henceforth no packaging, presentations, services, and products will get out to your customers that are not incredible.
- Select someone on your staff to be the "Quality Guard" if you are not personally able to oversee and inspect the quality of all the packaging, presentation, services, and products your company produces.
- Put weekly meeting times in your company's calendar with the sole purpose of asking, "Are our packaging, presentations, services, and products awesome yet? If not, what action steps do we need to take this week to get them to where they need to be?"
- Set up a quality control system that requires a signature from two "competent" people who have verified that the quality of everything is outstanding before going out to your customers.
- Set up a customer service survey program that aggressively solicits getting feedback from your customers. Offer to give your customers something, or a chance to win something, in exchange for filling out the survey. Make sure your survey asks the tough questions like, "On a scale of 1 to 10 (with 10 being the highest) how happy were you with the overall packaging of our products / services? On a scale of 1 to 10 (with 10 being the highest) how happy were you with the overall quality

of our products / services?" You must make sure that these questions involve getting a numerical response so that you can show patterns, quality drops, and quality improvements over time.

- Set up a system so that the customer feedback gets in front of the people designing your packaging, presentations, services, and products. This information must be presented factually and not sugar-coated with false kindness. They must know what customers sincerely think if they are going to be able to improve the overall value of your brand and the products and services your company provides.

MOVE #4 - Implement a merit-based program that pays your best people better than your worst people.

When Chester Cadieux started QuikTrip he did many things well while struggling to manage the daily operations. He expanded one convenience store at a time. As his company grew, he never lost his focus on providing the very best customer experience possible to each and every customer who came to QuikTrip. When people pumped gas, bought products, or used the restroom, he wanted them to experience cleanliness, organization, and friendliness. He wanted people to love their experience and over time he grew increasingly motivated to ensure that the level of customer service displayed in each store met his expectations. He simply could not handle the thought of the quality getting worse as the company expanded; as is the case with most businesses. To ensure the quality standards of his employees, he began utilizing "mystery shoppers." These secret shoppers came into the stores and bought things. They used the restrooms and purchased gas. The QuikTrip employees never knew they were there, but they did know that they would be getting paid based on how well they performed during these random inspections. Today, the company is still benefiting from the use of mystery shoppers and their merit-based program.

Basically, if employee A is acting like a jackass and employee B is doing a great job, their paychecks will be very different at the end of the month, year, and decade. If an employee does a bad job, they are quickly taught what they can do better and are given a chance to improve. If they keep working with the diligence of Charlie Sheen, they are fired. If they get with the program and begin offering great service, they get paid more. I know it's a crazy concept, but great work is actually valued more than bad work. At QuikTrip, an employee's performance actually determines the size of their pay check. View this system as Robin Hood in reverse. Essentially, you are taking from the poor to give to the rich. You are taking from the worst employees to give to the best employees.

Great employees love this system because it actually pays them what they are really worth. Great employees in systems like this consistently report loving the idea that the company simply will not tolerate poor performance. Managers around the country who work for companies where a merit-based pay system is in place report that much of the motivational aspects of management seem to simply take care of themselves when a merit-based pay system is in place. Put in a merit-based pay system and watch as the poor performers get irritated and leave; while the top performers become more and more eager to come to work every day in an environment that pays them what they are worth.

To make this system work for you, here is what you need to do:

- Develop a "secret shopper" program.
- Develop a "merit-based pay" program that systematically pays your top people more than your bottom people based upon the "secret shopper" reviews.

- Develop a system to publicly post everyone's "secret shopper" reviews so that a competitive spirit develops and people begin to benchmark themselves against the top people in your company.

MOVE #5 - Create an environment where "A Players" are celebrated, "B Players" are appreciated and "C Players" are shown the door.

When Jack Welch was the CEO of GE, he was able to produce record growth year after year by relentlessly using a few simple principles. The system of management he developed was called "Differentiation". This system was one of the key principles that energized GE and fueled the company's overall innovation and growth during his years as CEO of GE. At the core of the "Differentiation System" is a belief that everyone in every company should know where they stand in terms of their performance at all times. Long before Jack was appointed to the position of CEO for GE, he became convinced that "false kindness" and insincere feedback is the biggest dirty secret in business. As he climbed the corporate ladder during his early years at GE, he noticed that regardless where he was at in the company, "A, B, and C Players" acted in a consistent and predictable way.

He observed that "A Players" made up 20% of the work force. These people sincerely wanted to know how they were doing and how they could get better. He noticed that "A Players" were energized by positive change and couldn't seem to get enough of it. He also noticed that "B Players" made up 70% of the work force. These people desperately wanted to feel appreciated, valued, and respected. He noticed that "B Players" did not like change, but reluctantly fell in line once they were convinced that management was truly in favor of the change. Finally, he observed that "C Players" made up the bottom 10% of the company. He noticed these bottom-feeders could not handle candid feedback in the workplace and always became offended or emotionally hurt whenever they were told how they were doing and what they could do better. He noticed that "C Players" were consistently pessimistic, easily offended, chronically late, and always ready with a fresh batch of excuses why they could not get the job done. Thus, he devised a system that celebrated the "A Players" with kind words, public recognitions, bonuses, promotions, plaques, awards, and trophies. His system rewarded the "B Players" for their dependability and loyalty to the company. His incredible system also forced the underperforming "C Players" out the door and away from the GE family of businesses. This system worked for GE and it will work for your business too if you embrace the core principles.

To make this system work for you, here is what you need to do:

- Develop a system that ranks every employee on an A-C level in the following five categories:
    A. CORE JOB TASK - Their ability to do their core job description and work-related tasks well.
    B. EDGE - Their ability to get things done and make decisions regardless of whether it makes people upset or not.
    C. ENERGY - Their ability to bring energy to the workplace every day; whether they "feel good" or not.
    D. ENERGIZE - Their ability to ENERGIZE others in the workplace. Their ability to bring personal ENERGY to the workplace is very different from having the ability to ENERGIZE those around them.

    E. EXECUTE - Their ability to EXECUTE and to
       actually get things done, regardless of the
       circumstances around them.
  • Set aside time in your calendar for your team to let
    every employee know where they stand at every quarter
    of the fiscal year.
  • Develop a systematic way in which you will publicly
    celebrate your "A Players" and appreciate your "B
    Players".
  • Let your "C Players" know where they stand without
    any sugar-coating. Give them two weeks to improve
    and if they refuse, let them go. You must commit to
    firing the bottom 10% of your employees quarterly.

Move #6 - Create a fun workplace environment where your
employees share in the overall profitability of the company as a
whole.

When Herb Kelleher started Southwest Airlines, he didn't
have a lot of cash. He had enough cash to buy his first planes,
but his investment team immediately got entangled in a big
lawsuit with one of their competitors who planned to sue them
out of existence before they had even flown their first flight.
However, what Herb Kelleher *did* have was a highly-motivated
group of individuals who were 100% committed to seeing the
company succeed. His first employees were in the fight with
Herb. Herb wasn't fighting the fight alone. But why?
    Today, Southwest Airlines continues to be profitable.
However, now they are one of the few Airlines in the world
that is consistently profitable; but why? Is it their ability to
hedge the cost of fuel by buying fuel in mass quantities? Are
they profitable because they use "winglets" on their planes
which make planes 2-3% more fuel efficient? Are they
profitable because they don't charge for checking bags? Why

are those Southwest people so darn profitable when American Airlines can't seem to ever turn a profit?

Southwest consistently turns a profit because they have an employee ownership program that gives their employees a sense of ownership that is very real. When the company does well financially, the employees do well financially. When the company struggles, the employees struggle. In fact, this system has been proven to work so well that many of America's top companies use it as a motivational tool. It is also used as a means to share the wealth with the men and women who have worked hard day in and day out to make these companies profitable.

Think of the potential power just waiting to be unleashed at many companies. What if every employee was super-concerned about reducing the company's paper usage costs? What if every employee cared about reducing the company's electrical bill because it helps their paycheck? What if every employee was financially motivated to treat customers the right way? What if every person at your company was as obsessed as you are about watching the costs like a hawk? Would things change? Absolutely they would. The program that Southwest Airlines, QuikTrip, and other top companies have in place is called an ESOP program, which stands for an Employee Stock Ownership Plan.

To make this program work for you, here is what you need to do:

- 1. Look up ESOP attorneys in Google and find a few in your community.
- 2. Meet with them and convey your vision of sharing the profits (NOT THE GROSS REVENUE) with your employees. Ask them how much it would cost to set up a plan like this and then how they would recommend setting it up.

- 3. Read the Harvard Case Study / Book entitled, *The Service Profit Chain*, written by James L. Heskett, W. Earl Sasser, and Leonard A. Schlesinger. This book explains the ins and outs of this system and how companies like Outback, Southwest, and UPS are thriving because of the use of them.

**SUPER-IMPORTANT NOTE:

Remember to ask yourself, "Did these companies get big because of these systems or did they wait until they got big to set up these systems?" My friend, they set up these systems early on, which is why they got big.

Chapter Four

*BIG IDEA #4: Accept That Common Sense
Is No Longer Common*

To turn a profit you must begin to accept the fact that common sense is no longer common. You must set up systems that will ensure that many of your employees don't have to think as much as possible. You must be like the fast food companies which have actually set up a system for filling up small, medium, and large sized cups to decrease spillage. You must think more like the city of New York; which has decided it is now illegal for people to order a large sugary carbonated beverages because too many New Yorkers are drinking so many per day that they are now developing diabetes. You must post up labels on the side of HOT COFFEE POTS that say, "HOT TO THE TOUCH." You must put signs on your company microwaves that say, "EXPLOSION DANGER. DO NOT PUT SILVERWARE INTO THE MICROWAVE." You must find software that includes predictive text to prevent MASSIVE SPELLING ERRORS from going out to the masses. YOU MUST NOT EVER THINK THAT ANYTHING IS "COMMON SENSE" or you will soon find yourself BEING SUED BY AN IDIOT who was "UNAWARE THAT SILVERWARE COULD NOT GO INTO A MICROWAVE."

We now live in a society where school systems are taking hours and hours of study time to teach kids that if you they have sex with each other someone could get pregnant. My friends, I'll be the first to admit that I am not America's smartest man, but we are at an age of unprecedented American stupidity. Consider the fact that when *Newsweek Magazine* asked 1,000 American citizens who the Vice President of our country was, 29% were clueless to what his name. My friends, I recently had to conduct a quasi-workshop for employees of one of my companies who were unable to address an envelope correctly. Is it their fault that they are just clueless? At this point it really doesn't matter. The fact is that they now work for me and I'm going to have to take a proactive approach when it comes to teaching new employees how to mail things properly.

- **Verify the Insanity At:**
  http://www.thedailybeast.com/newsweek/2011/03/20/h
  ow-dumb-are-we.html

My friend, if you and I wanted to write a comedy movie about all of the things that employees have ever done, I'm sure we'd all have endless hilarious stories to tell. However, because we are trying to turn a profit, our stories are becoming modern tragedies. Trust me, I know that employees will do crazy things and when they do it's not funny at the time, or maybe even now. However, I also know that it is always funny to watch someone else get punched or kicked in the crotch. So I thought I would take a brief moment for comic relief to list a few crazy things my employees have done which has personally shown me how little "common sense" is left in America. These examples of idiocy have cost me a lot of money and time, yet I think they will be funny for you to read. To me they are just infuriating. Ladies and gentlemen, prepare to laugh as you witness me getting kicked in the crotch repeatedly at close range:

- **Excuse me sir, could you help me lift the heavy stuff?** After a wedding reception, one of my employees that had just DJ'ed actually walked up to the father-of-the-bride who had just witnessed his beautiful little princess and daughter's wedding day and said some variation of the following, "Um excuse me sir. It's really been an honor working with you tonight. Well anyway, this equipment is really heavy and I just wanted to see if you could help me carry out the big stuff to my car." Apparently, the Father of the Bride was so shocked by his request that he actually assisted our idiot DJ with the carrying his equipment. The Monday morning after the wedding, I found out from the venue the bride, guests, and mother-of-the-bride of the employee's idiocy. When I asked the employee what he was thinking he said, "Man, I was really tired and when I asked him he said yes. You know, come to think of it, I don't think that this topic was ever even really covered in our new hire handbook."

- **So I'm going through a divorce, but I hope your marriage works out.** I had one of my employees decide to open up and share about his recent divorce while engaging with the bride and the groom at their wedding. They said, "Hey thanks for entertaining tonight!" And he said, "Well, enjoy it while it lasts. Most marriages don't last you know. In fact, I'm recently divorced." When I asked him why he would say that kind of thing to a couple he said, "Well, I think they just needed to know where I was coming from and I'd rather be honest about how it really is man."

- **I need more hours, but could I take the next couple of days of?** I had one employee schedule a time to meet with me because he was "financially struggling". I knew what his paychecks were each week, so I wasn't sure why he was having financial difficulties, so I asked him, "What's going on?" He said, "I really am in pinch financially right now because of some things going on outside of work, so I could really use some extra hours." After I agreed to find some extra work for him to do, he then said, "Hey, I need to request off tomorrow and a couple of days next week to deal with some personal issues. And I already promised I would take tomorrow off for my wife's birthday."

- **I think it's more romantic when we meet with brides in the dark.** When our team meets with clients they are trained to have the presentation office looking clean, neat, and orderly. Well, we soon discovered that one of our employees had a whole different take on what it mean to keep the office "clean, neat, and orderly". We discovered that he liked to meet with all of the clients in the dark. Obviously, as soon as I found out I asked him, "What are you thinking man? What is going on in your head?" His response was classic. "Sir, I feel that if we meet with the brides in a setting with lower and more dim light it'll be more romantic."

- **Excuse me, I know you're 16, but could I date you?** We had to fire one employee for really going above and beyond. After a wedding reception we had one of our former DJ's ask a girl out on a date. He was 35. She was 16. She said no. Then the daughter of the bride told her mother (the bride) about the DJ's advances. When I subsequently found out about the situation from the post event survey, I asked the man what he was thinking and his response was pure insanity. He said, "Well, I wasn't going to do anything."

- **Look, I didn't mean to look at porn, I just wanted to update my Facebook status.** I did consulting with one restaurant that actually had to fire a guy for looking at pornography while checking out a customer at the register (no pun intended). When he confronted the employee about looking at pornography on his smartphone while collecting payment from a customer he responded, "I honestly didn't even know what site my phone was on. I just pulled it out to update my Facebook status."

- **Look, I'm paying child support for 3 people here; you've got to pay me more!** We had one employee who came to us and said, "You guys are not paying me enough and you guys are not treating me fairly or paying me what I'm worth. I can barely support myself." I responded by saying, "Well you make well over $1,000 per week. Where is your money going?" He said, "Well I've got another baby on the way and I'm already paying child support to two other ladies."

- **I do show up two hours late every day, but I do always show up.** At one of the companies I did consulting with, I had to advise the owner to fire one of their managers because "he was not setting a good example for his team and was not being diligent about completing his work related responsibilities." When we sat down to talk to him I said, "Brother, you show up to work two hours late per day. You don't help out your clients in a timely manner and you never respond to your emails or voicemails." He sincerely responded,

"Hey look, I don't know why you guys are treating me so unfairly. I do eventually show up every day."

- **I would like to work in your call center, but I refuse to make outbound calls.** At one company I did consulting for there were three team members who applied and were hired for a position working in a CALL CENTER. Within two weeks on the job the three of them had joined together in their refusal to make outbound calls. I arranged a meeting with them to confront the three and I said, "Hey ladies, what's going on with you all not making calls? I've heard you are actually refusing to make calls." One of the girls confidently responded by saying, "Well, I think we do better when we meet with people face-to-face." I had a hard time not laughing, but I responded and said, "When you applied a position in a call center, what did you think you were applying for?" Their idiocy was truly unbelievable to me.

- **I didn't know that I couldn't listen to music that contains endless expletives while working.** We hired one guy who lasted about two days at work that wore a shirt and tie as required by our dress code. Only he wore a hat with the tag still on it that he cocked to one side to show everyone at the office his allegiance to the "street life" while working. He then proceeded to wear basketball shoes with laces untied. I asked him, "Hey, why are you wearing a hat to the office? We have a shirt and tie environment." He said, "Oh, I didn't realize we couldn't wear a hat and basketball shoes with our dress clothes." The next day while working he was listening to gangster rap that was spewing out curse word after curse word in rapid succession. I told him to turn it off and he sincerely looked at me and said, "I didn't realize that we couldn't listen to music at work."

- **Look, no one ever told me that I couldn't spit sunflower seeds on the floor while working.** We had one employee who did great in every area of his job, but he would literally spit sunflower seeds on the floor in front of him while working. I told him to stop and he told me that "he was offended for always coming down on him about little things."

- **I can't believe that you are making me wear makeup and do my hair everyday I come to work.** During one meeting I was having with a client whom we were helping to turn around her business, we told all of the female and male employees that they would now need to follow the new presentation system when meeting with each client. We advised that we expected both the men and women to dress professionally when in front of the clients. One woman said defiantly, "Are you trying to tell me that I have to wear makeup and do my hair every day before coming to work?" I fired her on the spot because you just can't fix dumb.

My friend, moving forward as you continue hiring more and more people to accommodate the expansion of your company you must realize that you are going to have to start with the basics here. You and I can't go around frustrated all the time because we thought this or that was common sense. In order to be successful in your business endeavors, your team is going to have to devote some quality time to training people on things you thought were "common sense." In order to teach this "common sense" systematically you must take the following action steps.

Step 1 - Make an "Employee Handbook" that covers everything! This handbook should cover the following topics: Your company's overall mission statement and vision, appearance requirements, attendance expectations, the company's history, conflict resolution, employee hygiene requirements, grounds for termination, internet usage, pay expectations, sick day policies, smartphone usage, smoke break policies, what your company considers to be sexual harassment, and everything else that you think should be "common sense". You might even want to put a little reminder in there for everyone to brush their teeth every day. We once hired a sharp looking dude with a good resume who didn't quite seem to know that was required. If you need help drafting your company's handbook, please contact our team through our website at www.MakeYourLifeEpic.com and we will coach you through this terrible, mind-numbing, and soul-sucking process of stating the obvious so that you don't get sued when morons (one-third of the American workforce) do dumb things.

Step 2 - Make sure this book is as small as possible and that it is required reading for all of your employees.

Step 3 - Create a test that they must pass to prove that they have actually read the "Employee Handbook."

Step 4 - Have all of your employees sign a "Work Agreement" that states that they have read the "Employee Handbook," that they have passed a test about it, and that they know what is considered grounds for termination.

Chapter Five

BIG IDEA #5: Management = Mentorship

Management **equals mentorship** in a country where over 50% of the population has been raised in a home without parental supervision from two stable parents. By now we all know that the breakdown of the traditional American family is plaguing our country in endless ways. Countless news stories have been done about the social problems that society is beginning to experience as a result of the fatherless home epidemic. In fact, the National Fatherhood Initiative indicates 60% of America's rapists, 72% of adolescent murderers, and 70% of long-term prison inmates come from fatherless homes. As I travel around the country working with businesses both large and small, it is always shocking to me as I witness the reality of these social trends. This destruction of the American family is now destroying the American workplace as well.

Recently I had one employer ask me if he should allow his employees to curse in the workplace, because so many of them had come from homes where cursing was commonplace. I actually had one business owner ask me if he should change his company's timeliness policies because such a large percentage of his employees were chronically late. Countless employers ask me what is the best way to deal with employees who spend one-third of their day on their smart phones texting and updating their social media platforms. Apparently, these employees claim they need their phones for personal use in case of an emergency and that not allowing them to bring a smartphone to the workplace would be a violation of their rights. I personally dealt with an employee who hit on another employee in our office and actually had sex with them within the first 48 hours of meeting them. Then unbeknownst to me, the female employee involved in this situation posted on Facebook that the male employee involved in this situation was beating her and her two year old child. As an employer and entrepreneur what are we supposed to do in that situation? Where is the rule book for those types of situations?

Call centers I work with now tell me that many of their employees don't feel comfortable making calls and that making calls would give them an anxiety attack. Frankly, why should an employer care whether an employee feels comfortable about making calls? My friend, our society has given out so many eighth place trophies to kids who have never actually won anything that we now have a massive group of people who think they are incredible employees when, in fact, they have no discernible skills of value. It's amazing how many companies have told me that they struggle to find people who are willing to start entry level jobs. These companies and human resource directors have explained that it seems like every new employee "is looking for something in management," yet very few people are showing an ability to actually be "effectively managed".

HR Directors and small business owners throughout the country have told me that the majority of kids coming out of college or high school now feel like they are God's gift to every employer. Many of these business leaders have told me that over the past 20 years they have noticed a complete flip flop in certain aspects of the employee and employer relationship. In the 1970s, 1980s and 1990s employees were thankful that they had a job. Today, the majority of employees entering the workforce believe that their employers should be thanking them for finding the time to come to work each day.

Because the public school system is coddling every student, many young people now enter the workforce believing that they are the "chosen one" at their new place of employment. Employers are now witnessing recent college graduates who believe they should now be viewed as "trusted advisors". Immediately upon their arrival at their new jobs they believe that they are somehow smarter than their employers simply because they hold a college degree. To make matters worse, many colleges are allowing kids to opt-out of classes that they "struggle with". I know of two situations where that happened involving people I know directly. The college graduate bragged about convincing a major university to allow the student to pass a college course without being required to ever actually pass the exams; simply because they had concocted a believable "learning disability" for the first time in their lives which was now affecting their ability to study. These two men actually convinced the college that they were victims. They convinced the school they had "learning disabilities" that they were just now discovering that it "made it impossible for them to pass these courses". Furthermore, students over the past decade have effectively manipulated many colleges into believing that they were "doing their best" and that "denying them their right to a college degree would be a terrible thing to do". How is this crap possible? In both of these situations I knew that neither one of these two men ever studied. I knew that they never studied in high school either. However, in high school they were bright enough to pass the courses simply by being good guessers. However, because college was harder, they were unable to pass classes using their tricks. Thus, they quickly "discovered their learning disabilities". Earning a degree is not a right. Going to college is not a right. If you can't pass the test, you should fail.

And if you fail, you shouldn't be given a degree as some great big consolation prize.

Instead, many universities are out there are awarding degrees to anybody who qualifies for a federal student loan. And to make it worse, a 2011 article written by Michelle Flandreau and Kyle Schettler for *MSNBC* showed that student loan debt has surpassed credit card debt in size. According to data retrieved from the U.S. Department of Education, currently only about a third of student loan borrowers are even current on their payments. Thus, 13.8% of student loan borrowers have defaulted on their loans within three years of starting repayment. And this time bomb of loan defaults is set to explode any minute with endless numbers of students and graduates already benefiting from taking advantage of deferment or forbearance options. Essentially, we have approximately 15% of student loan borrowers defaulting on their loans and 66% of student loan borrowers who are not making payments on time. And now that all student loans are owned by the U.S. federal government, tax paying Americans like you and I are going to get stuck with the bill from the deadbeat debtors.

Now the only reason that these examples are appropriate for a book on managing effectively is because they demonstrate the kind of entitlement mindset that half of the workforce now brings to their first day on the job. They have a degree that many of them didn't work hard for and that was paid for by money that they never saved and they will never pay back. Now they want you to give them a good paying job because it's their right. Just a few generations ago, most American kids were aware that the Constitution gives us the rights to "life, liberty, and the pursuit of happiness." The Constitution doesn't even guarantee us happiness, because happiness is an individual decision. When you and I wake up each morning we get to decide what kind of day we are going to have. However, today's young people are being taught in school that if they are not happy it is someone else's fault and a doctor can prescribe them something that can help. If they can't pass a test, it's not their fault and the government will help. If they can't afford a phone, it's not their fault and the government will help. If they are fat, it's not their fault and the government will stop the mean and terrible fast food companies from taking advantage of them. Nothing is ever their fault; it's always the fault of somebody else. These people are being taught that there are absolutely no consequences for their actions. However, the world of business is very different.

In the world of business, we do directly experience the consequences for our actions. If we make great products, customers come back and buy from us time and time again. In the world of business it's black and white and it is our fault if the client is not happy. If our company delivers a crappy product or service, it is our company's fault and the customer will choose to buy from someone else. And no, nine times out of ten they won't give us a second chance. In business, if we are late our customers will get irate and then they will buy from our competitors. Consumers don't care about what "personal problems" we are having at home. In business if we can't get the product and service done right, our customers, who do not care about our learning disabilities, will simply take their money and their business somewhere else that can get it right. And that is the "great debacle" that many American businesses are beginning to experience in epidemic proportions. How can you grow a business with a workforce filled with people who have never been asked to be accountable for their actions? How do you grow a business with an army of employees who believe they can't do a pushup because of the evil fast food companies, who can't take criticism because they believe they are victims, and who believe they can't show up on time because of the personal issues they are having at home? That is what we're now going to tackle with two simple rules.

Rule #1 - Diligently assess potential employees before you hire them. If they are not already "A Players" or "B Players"-don't hire them. If you thought someone was an "A Player" or a "B Player" and you soon find out that they are in fact a "C Player" soon after hiring them, fire them. Refer "C Players" to a church, a counselor, the Job Corps, the military, or somebody who is willing to kick their butt until they get their life together; but don't waste your time trying to life coach bottom feeders into becoming productive citizens. Your business exists to produce great products, service, and profits. Your business simply cannot afford to invest time in slackers and people who have alibis for their excuses and justifications for their failures. I always tell my people, "Don't hire people who suck at life."

Rule #2 - Mentor your "A Players" and "B Players." Understand that most of the people you are hiring didn't have a good family life or a school system that made them accountable for anything. However, somehow these people made it through the system and have become functional humans that are not slackers. This, in and of itself, deserves some praise. However, because these employees didn't have good mentorship growing up they are going to need to get mentorship from you. And they are going to need to get it in 4 ways:

    1) Modeling - You are going to have to model the behavior that you want your employees to display. If you want your employees to be polite, you are going to have to be polite. If you want do not want them to be late, YOU CAN NEVER BE LATE. If you want them to read books, you are going to have to read books. Most of today's employees simply will not follow the rules just because you say they should do so. They

will follow the rules if you earn their respect and if they know why the rules are in place. Respect for leadership is no longer a given in today's society where kids are allowed to talk back to their parents. You must hold yourself accountable to a higher standard if you want your employees to follow your systems and instructions.

2) Public Praise - You must catch your employees doing something well. Because these people have all been coddled and shielded from consequences, they emotionally cannot process constructive criticism the way that they should. Thus, to get them to be receptive to the feedback you and clients give, you must look for reasons to praise them for the good things that they actually do. Whenever they do something well-smile, shake their hands, high-five them, beat a drum, or just do something to share with everyone how good of a job they did.

3) Assign Required Reading - Today's employees can update their social media on their smartphones and can probably control a space station from their personal computer, but most of them struggle with reading, writing, comprehension, and critical thinking skills. Essentially, they are unable to study successful people or systems that work and apply these principles into their own lives. Thus, you can't assume that they are even able to understand what your company memos mean as it relates to them. Many employees have hidden behind their computer screens so long that they now struggle to verbally express themselves in an effective manner. Assign these books for your people to read and hold them accountable to reading them and your business culture will exponentially improve:

- o *How To Win Friends and Influence People* - by Dale Carnegie
- o *The World's Greatest Salesman* - by Og Mandino
- o *Who Owns the Ice House?* - by Clifton Taulbert

4) Candid Feedback Presented With Love - You must let your employees know that you are on their team and that you are 100% committed to seeing them develop into great people. John Maxwell, the leadership guru, said, "People don't care how much you know until they know how much you care." This is true. And your people will simply not listen if they think your focus is only on the business tasks. Most of these people have grown up in small families where their opinion was super important. The majority of them have been told by every guidance counselor in the world, "You are special and you have great potential!"

When you tell your employees they did something wrong, this information will rock their minds. The school system has never forced most students to ever be accountable for anything and now you are asking them to take ownership of a problem they caused. This concept might very well break the brain of many employees. Remember, most have been told that if they are fat, it is the evil fast food company's fault. They've been told if they don't do well in school it's because they have a learning disability; or if they fail to earn a good job out of college it's the education system's fault. Trust me on this. This concept has the potential to absolutely demoralize some people. We actually had one woman that worked for us who took terrible photos during training and her trainer told her that "her photos needed a lot of work" and she cried. Then after she got it together and composed herself she started crying again. Then she wrote me a super long Facebook message explaining to me that she simply "could not work in an environment where her trainer was so mean." In an office environment I've literally witnessed dozens of people cry when they were told by their supervisor that their work needed improvement in some areas.

When you give your people feedback, you must let them know that first and foremost you are committed to helping them succeed as a person; and you must mean it. You must hug before you kick. Don't candy-coat your feedback; just make sure you go out of your way to tell them that you care before giving them candid feedback.

To make mentorship work for you, here is what you need to do:

1) Commit yet again to not hiring "C Players." Tell your kids, tell your wife, tell your team, and tell everybody that "C Players" will not work for you.
2) Let up a "Buddy System" at work in which all new employees have to shadow someone who sets a good example for how to do things the right way.
3) Put a line item into your weekly staffing meetings to "Publicly Praise" people who did a great job during the past week.
4) Put the required reading materials into your "New Hire Employee Packet" and set up a strong reward for reading them (a cash bonus) and a strong penalty (a cash fine) for not reading them.

Chapter Six

BIG IDEA #6: Candor Must Be a Constant

I f you are going to effectively manage you must have the ability to be candid. Your employees must know that you do not have the ability to dish out false kindness or bogus compliments. Your employees must know that when you compliment them or their work, you mean it. They must also know that when you offer constructive criticism and feedback you also mean it. Candor must be a constant if you are truly committed to producing great profitability through the creation of tremendous products and services. Before we get into this candor topic, let's take a second out to define what candor truly means. According to Webster and his band of merry men, candor means, "the state or quality of being frank, open, and sincere in speech or expression." Basically, you are being candid if you are telling people the truth at all times; whether they want to hear it at the time or not.

Whether I'm consulting in Miami or Denver, lack of candor is a huge problem in businesses everywhere. This is because most people confuse being tactful with not telling the real truth if it has the potential to make someone upset. So to help you deal with the candid truth that 90% of you reading this are not being candid enough, I will give you three examples of real life business situations I found myself pulled into during the early portion of my business career; before I had the management skills and mental maturity needed to be candid. You can laugh at me here. Then I will give you three examples of business situations where I did have the courage and management maturity to be candid and you can see how you should be using candor in the workplace.

Managing <u>Without</u> Candor
Example 1: We once had an employee working for us who was almost not understandable on the phone. His speech was filled with so much rapper slang and broken speech that all clients rejected him just because they had no idea what the crap he was talking about. Because I wanted "to be nice," I kept telling him, "Hey man, just stay positive and you will eventually get one." Each week he would set appointments with people who would never show up. The few appointments he did get to show up were hopelessly poor and came to the appointments just to get the FREE stuff. Because I didn't have the courage needed to be candid, I could never bring myself to telling him that he sounded like a member of the Wu-Tang Clan and not like a wedding planner.

Because I didn't have enough courage to be candid with him he struggled and eventually quit because he couldn't afford not to. He worked with us for three months or so and never experienced any success. It was my fault for not being candid with him. It was weak and, therefore, his results were weak.

Managing <u>With</u> Candor
Example 1: After learning and embracing the concept of courageously using candor at all times, I ran across an employee who was working for one of my consulting clients. The employee was not from this country. Every time she talked her voice screamed, "Hey potential buyers, I am from another country!" Every time she made a call, prospects would hang up on her because they obviously felt like she was a telemarketer calling from a third-world country. I sat her down and told her,

"Hey Kim (we'll use this name to protect her identity). Your effort is there. Your energy is there. You even sound articulate on the phone; however, every time you call someone they are thinking, *'Hey this person is from another country. They must just be some telemarketer. I'm going to hang up.'* So to fix this situation, when someone picks up the other line I want you to say, 'Hey is this such and such'? And when they answer I want you to say, 'Hi, this is Kim and I'm actually from Brazil. How are you tonight?'"

Nearly every time she said that, most people said, "Really, so why are you calling me?" They actually talked to her instead of hanging up on her. This got the conversation going to the point that she could actually experience some success. If I hadn't told her that her accent was devastatingly affecting her calls, she would have had no success. Sure, she wouldn't have been offended, but she would have been depressed by all of the rejections.

Managing <u>Without</u> Candor
Example 2: Long before I learned to be candid, I had a guy that worked with us who always showed up late to work. He would always apologize for being late, and I would always act like I was forgiving him. But without any exaggeration, he was late at least two-thirds of the time he was supposed to come to work. Over time I got extremely irate with him, but I never told him because I was weak and "I didn't want to hurt his feelings". He continued being late and I continued being irate.

Eventually, as we grew it became time to promote someone to the position of manager. I promoted someone else and he was devastated. He said, "Dude, I've been here for years. I've always been the top sales guy and now you are promoting someone else?! That is crazy. I feel like I'm getting stabbed in the back."

I responded by saying, "Dude you have been late nearly every day during your entire career, there is absolutely no way I could ever promote you until you have shown that you can be diligent and dependable about managing your time and the simple act of being on time!"

He then said, "Look, if I had known it was a problem, I would have fixed it a long time ago. I thought it was just one of those things that was no big deal."

Again, in this situation, my lack of candor hurt the employee and the business. Because I was too weak to say something for fear of "hurting his feelings" I hindered his development and built up an animosity for this person that he was unaware of; until it became time to promote someone to management and he didn't get the job. Trust me; we all owe it to our people to be candid with them at all times.

Managing With Candor
Example 2: I had an employee consistently showing up to work late. We now have a system that fines people every time they are late. These fees then are redistributed as a bonus to the "most valuable employee of the week". After a couple of days of being late and being fined, I told the employee that if they ever wanted to be promoted or to advance in life in any way, they were going to have to develop a reputation for being on time. When I told her, she looked at me and appeared shocked. She said, "I had no idea that was such a big deal. I'm so sorry."

Almost immediately the tardiness and chronic lateness stopped. This employee went from being someone who had no shot at being promoted to being one of our top people within just a few short months. Ultimately, employees can choose how they are going to respond to the feedback you give them in their own way. Some will take the information you give them to heart. Some people will sincerely care about what you are saying. Others will choose to become offended, which will ultimately result in their exit from your company. Leave that choice up to them, but do the right thing and be candid.

To make candor work for you, here is what you need to do:

1) Commit to always telling employees sincerely what you think about them at all times.
2) Commit to always attacking poor performance and not people when you are forced to deliver negative feedback, news, or performance reviews.
3) Set up a quarterly employee performance review session with all of your employees and make candor your top priority in these meetings.

Chapter Seven

BIG IDEA #7: Inspect, Never Expect

We've all heard the phrase, "never assume, because when you do it makes an ass out of you and me". Well, this phrase has never been truer than when you are managing people or money. In order to manage effectively in a country where situational morality is now the norm and the majority of the people no longer worry about any eternal consequences for their earthly actions, you must assume everyone is lying to you at all times. In order for you to succeed you are going to have to set up weekly times at which you or some of the rare people that you can actually trust must inspect each element of your company's workflow to make sure it is being done right. You might have a great business plan and great systems in place. But your business will struggle mightily if you or a trusted individual are not taking time out each week to inspect that the things you expect for your employees to do are done correctly.

President George Washington once said, "I cannot tell a lie" but your most recent hire is not former President George Washington. In every business, both large and small, that I have consulted with, I have discovered that things have a way of slipping through the cracks if there is not an accountability system in place to monitor the behavior and activities of all individuals. In fact, I am so confident in this concept of "Inspect, Never Expect" that I would strongly advise you to work off the assumption that everyone is lying. Work off the assumption that I am lying now. Assume that everything that is not provable in this book is bogus. Do your research and if you find credible information validating what I am saying, then you should accept it as truth. If the information I'm saying cannot be proven, then work off of the assumption that what I am saying is wrong. By doing this you will save yourself a lot of personal heartache and frustration. More importantly, you will end up developing incredible accountability systems that will allow your business ensured success and growth. Show me a company that does not have systems in place to verify the adherence to high quality standards in their products and services and I will show you a company that is financially struggling or is on the verge of collapse.

Think for a moment about all of the truly incredible brands. Picture them in your mind. As an example, picture Disney World in your mind's eye. They see millions and millions of customers every day and yet the overwhelming majority of their guests report having an incredible experience with each and every visit to the theme parks. Yet, in small and medium-sized businesses throughout the country, we struggle to maintain a high-quality standard. In fact, the more customers they have, the worse the quality gets. Thus, we now have a ton of business owners walking around our communities saying crazy things like, "Well, I'm trying to keep my business small so that I can keep the quality high." What kind of nonsense thinking is this? If being small meant being the best, then Apple would have had one employee who is now dead.

If this kind of thinking has been limiting the growth of your company then you simply must begin to change your thinking immediately. You must begin saying, "Our company is going to offer the best quality on the planet and we are going to be massive."

After speaking at one event in New Mexico, I was approached by the disk jockey that was going to be entertaining the guests after their day spent learning. He wore a very sharp brown suit and was well groomed. He seemed sincere in his questioning, so I had no reason to suspect that his brain was in fact four times smaller than that of the average human. Because of the way he looked and the way he approached me, I had no reason to believe that he had less vision than a blind mind. However, after about four sentences, I was convinced that this guy was in need of a complete lobotomy.

He said, "Excuse me Clay; I heard you speak and I wanted to ask you a couple of quick questions." I said, "Sure, boss, how can I help you?" He then replied, "Well I own a DJ company and I know that you started one of the nation's largest wedding entertainment companies. So I guess I was wondering, how you are ok with sacrificing quality for growth?"

I looked at him and gave him what probably appeared to be the Darth Vader look of death, but I kept myself composed while speaking. I replied, "Could you repeat the question, I guess I don't understand what you're talking about?" He confidently said, "Well, you know I'm really focused on quality so I personally do the events myself and I have two other guys I can trust." I said, "Well that's great." He said, "Well you know, I heard you speak and I've always wondered how people like you can justify sacrificing quality for quantity." I then realized that this man was the dumbest man on the planet. I figured that I should take at least thirty seconds to force feed him some meaningful thoughts and concepts into his otherwise empty head. I replied, "Boss, how long have you been DJ'ing?" He happily replied with a big grin on his face, "I've been doing this for over 25 years. Yeah, sometimes it's hard to believe how time flies by.." I then said, "Man, we are looking at the world from two very different perspectives. You are assuming that if you are big your quality has to go down and I am 100% sure that it is a proven fact that your quality has to rise dramatically as you increase in size if you are to succeed. Apple has made incredible products and Steve Jobs wasn't some dude personally making computers out of his living room for the past 20 years. Sure, he and Woz started out of the garage, but they didn't stay there because they wanted to maintain a high quality standard. Sure, Walt Disney started out doing his own animation, but as Disney grew he delegated and eventually churned through enough people until he found some animators that were as good, or better, than he was. Man, what's the point of even owning a business if you are going to aim for something so small? You've got to get serious about adding as much value to the planet as possible if you are going to make a dent in the universe and actually make some real money." He retorted, "Well that's easy for you to say, you don't have to deal with the kind of horrible employees I have to deal with."

I realize again that this guy did not want help or to get the answers to his questions; he just wanted to complain about life. He seemed to hate his life, yet didn't have the courage to try to do things differently in an attempt to get a different result. I sincerely think that guy just didn't understand that whole concept of cause and effect. Don't start sounding like this guy. If you do sound like this guy currently, take a moment to pull your head out of your butt. Life will smell much sweeter.

So in order to help you build the ultimate business machine that is capable of growing in massive qualities, you are going to need to get to work creating the following accountability systems:

- Develop a system to verify how much time your team is actually spending marketing your products and services.

- Develop a system to verify that your website is being optimized and updated correctly.
- Develop a system to verify what percentage of your leads comes from your various marketing activities.
- Develop a system to verify that your team is answering the phone correctly.
- Develop a system to verify that your pricing and package structures are being followed.
- Develop a system to verify that emails are being sent out correctly and in the right format.
- Develop a system to verify that your services and products are physically being delivered on time and in good condition.
- Develop a system to verify that your clients are happy with the products and services you provide.
- Develop a system for reimbursements so that you know you are only paying for items and services that were actually purchased for business use.

My friend, you must develop a verification system for anything in your business that you expect to happen. You must inspect everything that you expect to happen. And what you accept will become what you should expect. Marinate on those deep thoughts for awhile and then start taking some action steps to make sure that you have proper accountability systems in place.

Chapter Eight

BIG IDEA #8: Fire Those Whom You Cannot Inspire

I f you are going to run a successful business you are going to have to be committed to your customers 100% of the time. These people are your boss and should be revered as such. What they say goes. You must absolutely become committed to listening and learning from your customers. If your customers begin to tell you that they don't like a certain product or service that you offer or an employee that you have working for you, you must be willing to act based upon their feedback if you find it to be factual. Simply put, if they say that your employee treated them rudely or didn't seem to care about them, you have a problem. However, you have a bigger problem if you refuse to take action because you are 100% committed to the assumption that your employees are right 100% of the time.

This concept was very tough for me to learn early on in my business career because I thought that everyone was a "good person" and that some employees "just needed some more time" or that some employees "were just going through some stuff". I am personally responsible for limiting our company's growth early on because I simply was unwilling to fire the people whom I could not inspire. And to make problems worse, I only fellowshipped with other small business owners who encouraged me to "stay committed to your people, they will eventually turn around." They would say other things like, "You know a lot of customers out there are just wackos!" However, as I began to ponder their feedback and the advice they were giving me I began to ask myself, "Do I really want to be like them? Do I really want to be 55 years old and still running a small and crappy business with zero growth potential? Do I really want to be stuck without any potential for business growth just because a few employees are unwilling to move to Dallas? Do I really want to not create an amazing customer experience just because a few employees are simply unwilling to follow the system every time?"

The Top Four Reasons Most Small To Medium Sized Businesses Will Not Fire People Whom They Cannot Inspire:

1. They're Good Friends - What makes it tough in the world of small business is that everyone starts to become friends over time. We start to feel bad inside because we know that when we fire someone, we are going to have to fire our first employee or the person who first helped us to develop our systems. We start to hold on to feelings of nostalgia. We start to remember the "good old days" when we first started growing the company together; and we feel trapped. This is flawed thinking. Remember you never truly fire anybody when you are candid about your employee's lack of performance. They are simply choosing not to conform to your policies and to do things the right way. They are forcing you to fire them. Remember, God did not feel guilty when he kicked Adam and Eve out of Eden. God is not currently going to some angelic counselor to deal with the guilt associated with judging others. My friend, judge your employees in terms of their work performance and be candid. If you don't, your customers certainly will.

2. We're Too Busy Right Now - You'll have to wait until after the busy season. When you own and/or operate any business that is not yet huge, you are always in a busy season and one person short. Personally, I have found that the larger we have gotten, the easier it has become to manage, hire, and fire. It's when you are small and mid-sized that things are tough. It's tough to fire a sales person who refuses to work as though he is inspired when you only have two sales people. It's really tough to fire 50% of your workforce. Trust me, I know. But everyday that you keep that underperforming and non-inspired employee working for you, they are doing you damage. They are convincing potential customers not to do business with you because of their bad attitude. They are taking up a spot on your roster that you could give to someone else that is a better employee with a better work ethic and a bigger desire to succeed. Regardless of how busy you are, you have to fire underperformers as soon as possible. You have to take action to get those weeds out of your business garden.

3. Their Kids Will Starve - You don't want to make anyone's family starve. Yet again friend, these feelings of guilt are not healthy when you are dealing with the firing of a negligent employee. Remember the employee is the one choosing to bring a lack of motivation to the workplace, not you. Remember because you are now candid with everyone, they know exactly where they stand and they have known for some time that they are doing a poor job when it comes to work performance. If they actually resort to using their family as hostages to guilt you into continuing their employment, then they are a sick freak and a bad employee.

No person with a fully functional soul would be willing to intentionally perform at a substandard level when they have a wife or kids to support. Although I don't understand the mindset of anyone who intentionally does a poor job at work, I really don't understand how anyone with a family they are supporting could intentionally do a terrible job at work. The only problem here is that some people don't have a fully functional soul. Some people don't care. Some people do not have personal pride. In this society in which we live, we are constantly told that we are wrong if we judge people. From an eternal perspective, it is true that only God can judge them. However, from an earthly perspective, we all judge people. The moment we meet somebody for the first time, we make a quick snap judgment about whether we like the person or not. There are countless studies and endless research that has proven this to be the case. Stop feeling bad if you have to judge an employee as doing a bad job. You are not saying, "You are bad person." You are simply saying, "You are doing such a bad job so consistently that we are now being forced to fire you because you are choosing not to improve."

4. The Fallout Will Kill Us All! - You're worried about what will happen when the employee leaves. I have met countless entrepreneurs who simply struggle to fire someone whom they know must be let go because they are worried about what will happen. In their mind they keep thinking, *if I say this, then they'll say that. If they say that, then it'll escalate and I'll say that as well.* My friend, to make it easy, let me break it down for you like this.

- IF YOU DO NOT FIRE THIS PERSON, YOUR CUSTOMERS ARE GOING TO FIRE YOU AND YOUR TOP PEOPLE WILL LEAVE BECAUSE THEY CAN'T STAND THE SIGHT OF MEDIOCRITY.
- IF YOU DO FIRE THEM, THIS CRAPPY EMPLOYEE MIGHT GO OUT AND GO TO WORK FOR YOUR COMPETITION; IN WHICH CASE YOU WILL BENEFIT BECAUSE YOU JUST GAVE YOUR DISEASE TO SOMEONE ELSE AND NOW YOU ARE DISEASE FREE.
- IF YOU DO FIRE THEM, THIS BAD EMPLOYEE WITH A CHRONICALLY BAD WORK ETHIC WILL SOON GO AND TELL HIS OR HER FRIENDS WHO

KNOW THEM AS BEING SOMEONE WITH A BAD WORK ETHIC, HOW TERRIBLE YOU ARE. BECAUSE BIRDS OF A FEATHER TEND TO FLOCK TOGETHER, THERE IS NO LOSS THERE.

- IF YOU DO FIRE THEM, LET'S ASSUME THAT THIS PERSON HAS GREAT FRIENDS WHO HAVE A SOLID WORK ETHIC. SOLID PEOPLE KNOW THAT GREAT COMPANIES DO NOT MAKE A HABIT OF FIRING GREAT PEOPLE. ALL QUALITY PEOPLE HAVE ENOUGH DISCERNMENT TO KNOW THAT EMPLOYEES ARE NOT FIRED FOR BEING GREAT; THEY ARE FIRED FOR BEING TERRIBLE EMPLOYEES.

5. Fear of Confrontation - If you simply can't muster up the courage to fire someone, know you are not alone. But you are weak. If this is the case and you are a business owner, you are in trouble. If this is your problem, you are either going to have to hire someone who has the courage of their convictions to fire someone. Or, you are going to have to accept that fact that your business and your life are going to be awful because you lack courage. If this is your problem, now is the time to MAN UP and make it happen. Get serious about your life and take control.

"Control your destiny or somebody else will." - Jack Welch (Former CEO of GE)

Chapter Nine

BIG IDEA #9: You Choose To Win or Lose

N ow that you know what to do, it all comes down to you. Will you take action? Or will you just say, "That was a good book with some interesting points in it." Will you embrace the concept that success is a choice? Or will you rely on wishing and hoping? If you decide right here and now that your business is going to be wildly successful, then your business will prosper. If you put this book down and say to yourself, "I hope this works" then it won't work.

My friend, doubt is the opposite of faith and the two cannot exist together in the same time and place. Either you believe or you don't. To build your faith and to absolutely hammer home the incredible importance of embracing the reality that success is a choice, I am going to give you one story of success that I've seen unfold right in front of my own eyes (as opposed to your eyes). However, before you begin reading these stories you must know that they all started with someone who decided to become wildly successful.

The "Good Life" - The Story of Ryan Tedder

On June 26th, 1979 Ryan Benjamin Tedder was born. Just like other babies he cried and needed to be taken care of by his mother. He was completely dependent. However, unlike most humans born that year, Ryan would later make the decision that he was going to make it in the music business as a performer and songwriter. Because I had the privilege of living on the same wing of the same college dormitory at Oral Roberts University as Ryan, I was able to see first hand what hard work and dedication looked like.

After class most people in college spend their time playing video games and mindlessly filling time with idle social activities. However, Ryan chose a different path. Each day whenever I would walk past his dorm room in route to the elevators, I would hear him and his guitar. He wasn't playing video games or talking about nothing for long periods of time because he was busy turning himself into a music guru. He was constantly singing and playing with an intensity that was unmatched. It was almost as if he had already been hired to work as a full-time musician in a big production studio.

While he was hard at work, I was starting a business out of my dorm room and I often would pull all-nighters because I simply ran out of time to get my homework and my business-related work done. After toiling away alone for several hours in my room, I would often walk down the hall to the community restroom. And although the rest of dormitory had usually gone quiet by this time, I would more often than not still hear Ryan singing and playing his guitar down the hall.

Ryan attended the same church (Christian Chapel) as several guys on the dormitory floor so we were all friends. We knew that Ryan's father was a Christian songwriter and that Ryan's mom was a wonderful school teacher and mother. We also knew that Ryan began playing the piano at age three as a result of instruction he had received. We all knew that Ryan was interested in music; yet I believe sincerely that very few people actually believed that Ryan was going to make it as a pop star and songwriter. However, I don't believe that Ryan cared too much about the opinions of others. This man was determined and focused on doing whatever it took to make it.

From his freshman to senior years in college, Ryan became increasingly focused on becoming the best musician he possibly could. Since the age of twelve Ryan had began teaching himself how to become a world-class vocalist, but by his sophomore year, the guy was laser beam focused on learning to really sing. He spent hours in his dorm room listening to and imitating Stevie Wonder, Peter Gabriel, Sting, other artists who could really sing. Day after day this guy worked at honing his craft.

Ryan worked as a server at various restaurants to support himself and to help make some extra money so that he could buy himself all of the recording equipment.. He seemed to view work as a means to an end; and his end was making it in the music business.

During the summers Ryan went to Nashville to relentlessly pursue an internship. Oddly enough he wasn't being recruited by these top record companies. HE HAD TO CHOOSE TO BECOME SUCCESSFUL. Ryan wasn't deterred by the lack of mega interest in his skills. He worked at Pottery Barn as a shop assistant while he worked to land an internship. Eventually he landed an internship with Dreamworks, SKG. There Ryan did whatever he had to do to create his own breaks into the industry. He offered to sing on demos and to help produce demo tracks for songwriters, labels, and other musicians. Tedder usually charged $300 to $400 per track and he would often times bring back the demos to college for us all to hear.

I remember playing his tracks for a few people who said, "Dude people with talent are a dime a dozen." It was their way of doubting him to make themselves feel better for not pursuing their passion. I know that Ryan undoubtedly heard the skepticism of others, but for some reason I believe it motivated him to press on.

At the age of twenty one, after spending multiple years essentially working without compensation, Ryan DECIDED to compete in a singer-songwriter competition that was being sponsored by MTV by 'N Sync singer and member Lance Bass. Ryan was one of only five finalists who got to perform on MTV as part of a one-hour special. Because Ryan had been practicing all day and all night for years, he was ready when his opportunity came. What a lot of people fail to see here, though, is that the opportunity did not just present itself to Ryan. Ryan had to physically move out of his comfort zone and into a big city swarming with artists who also had talent and musicians who also dreamed of mega music deals. But Ryan was different; he decided that he would succeed. He was willing to work for free as an intern and he was willing to apply for countless competitions until he finally created his own big break. Where would he have been if he had just waited for his phone to ring?

Well, Ryan performed and he won. Lance Bass was there to congratulate him with a recording contract. Ryan's performance of his song entitled, "The Look" captivated the audience and the audience responded by voting for him. Although things seemed to be looking bright for Ryan, the bottom fell out. It turned out that Lance's recording contract was not real and that it was really just a bunch of hype. Soon Lance's record label ceased to exist, but Ryan's fiery passion for making it big was not extinguished. However, undeterred, Ryan just kept marching on. If you look up "*On My Way Here* + Ryan Tedder" on YouTube you can find a song he wrote that describes his journey to the top. This song was also later performed by American Idol star, Clay Aiken.

Although Ryan's contract with Lance Bass ended up being a bunch of bunk, his performance did catch the attention of many "big time" people including, Timbaland, the Mega-Producer for Justin Timberlake, Missy Elliot, Flo' Rida and countless pop / R&B stars. Thus, during 2002-2004 Ryan went to work for Timbaland as an intern. During his time with Timbaland, Ryan got to see the music industry up-close for what it really was. He was able to produce tracks for artists while developing as an artist himself. The work that Tedder produced during this time crossed nearly every musical genre including hip-hop, R&B, rock, dance/techno, pop, and country.

Since that time Ryan has written countless songs for artists that are household names for most American and many families worldwide. In fact, Ryan has written songs for Adele, OneRepublic (his own group), Paul Oakenfold, Maroon 5, Gym Class Heroes, Far East Movement, Kelly Clarkson, B.O.B., Blake Lewis, Adam Lambert, Leona Lewis, Jordin Sparks, Gavin Degraw, Colbie Callet, and Beyonce. His first big worldwide hit was "Apologize." This song was the best-selling song of 2008 and broke U.S. records for most Radio Airplay with 10,331 spins in one week alone. He then followed that up by writing, "Bleeding Love" for Leona Lewis that broke the records previously set by "Apologize." He's written even more hits for the Backstreet Boys, Jennifer Lopez, Mario, DJ Tiesto, Ludacris, Jennifer Hudson, Carrie Underwood, Bubba Sparxxx, and the late Whitney Houston.

Today Ryan writes the hits for the stars. His songs continue to appear on the music charts and Billboard's Top 40 List. He's written pop hits such as, "Brighter Than the Sun" by Colbie Caillat, "Fighter" by the Gym Class Heroes, "Halo" by Beyonce, and "Secrets" which was recorded by his own group, OneRepublic. And Ryan is not done yet. In fact, if you look him up on Wikipedia, I'm sure he's produced songs for countless other big time stars that are not listed above.

He has now set up his own recording studio, record label, and distribution deal for the songs he writes and performs. One of Ryan's life long goals was to perform with U2 and recently he accomplished this goal. And despite Ryan's success, the harsh reality is that none of this would have been possible if he did not hold himself accountable for achieving his dreams. If he did not hold himself accountable to his self prescribed regimen of singing 2 hours per day, he would not have "made it." If he had not been willing to move to Nashville, Tennessee he would not have made it. If he would not have been willing to work / intern for free while working at the Pottery Barn, he would not have made it. Ryan achieved and succeeded because he simply decided to. Be like Ryan. Make the decisions to become successful and don't stop working until you get there. In a song he wrote and that was recorded by OneRepublic entitled "Marching On," Ryan describes his passion for overcoming adversity by singing a line that I love, "I sink us to swim, we're marching on."

My friend, until next time, remember Napoleon Hill's quote, "The time will never be just right, you must act now."

Bonus blank page for "compulsive drawing and note-taking."

Bonus blank page for "compulsive drawing and note-taking."

Bonus blank page for "compulsive drawing and note-taking."

Bonus blank page for "compulsive drawing and note-taking."

www.ingramcontent.com/pod-product-compliance
Lightning Source LLC
Chambersburg PA
CBHW031905200326
41597CB00012B/535